MW01130463

I Am
an Artist

Doro Globus and Rose Blake

David Zwirner Books

For Dorothea

What is an ARTIST and how do they work? Why do they make things? Can I be an artist?

Let's find out more!

An artist is someone who is creative and shares what they make with others. Artists can work with all types of materials and techniques—no two are the same. This building is full of people making all kinds of art (and messes) in their own spaces, called studios.

Viola

Kit

I wonder who is around today.
Kit, let's see if we can find some answers to your questions!

I am an artist who loves people. The longer I stare at a face, the more I notice who the person is on the inside. Sometimes I worry that the person gets uncomfortable or tired while I'm painting them, but I try not to let that bother me. When I paint portraits, I can tell a person's story.

Paintbrush

Easel

Apron

Bench

I am a portrait painter.

Tubes of paint.

We are artists who are always learning and practicing our techniques. You have to look closely at things to understand them or to find beauty in them, even if they are something really familiar, like a banana or a flower.

We all have our own way of seeing — it is amazing how different our drawings are even though we are looking at the same setup of objects, which is sometimes called a still life.

Table easel

Paper

Charcoal

Pencil

Pastels

Pineapple

Flowers

Backdrop

Candle

Mug

We are illustrators.

I am an artist who works with light and chance. My camera gives me the power to freeze time; I love that no two moments are ever the same. The magic really happens in the darkroom, when I print a photo. Using an enlarger, I project light through a piece of film onto special paper. Next I dip the paper into three different chemicals and the image appears.

How crazy is that?

Print tongs

Print trays

Chemicals

Darkroom

Drying line

Safelight

Film

Enlarger

Timer

I am a photographer.

I am an artist who loves color, but I don't have a favorite! I like that everyone sees color in different ways. Making sculptures out of metal is a big, heavy job, but I have a team of talented people who help me.

Sculptures

I hope the colorful shapes I make bring happiness to spaces and joy to the people who experience them.

I am a sculptor.

I am an artist with a passion for moving images. I like creating imaginary worlds. I start with a small, simple idea that I grow into something big and exciting.

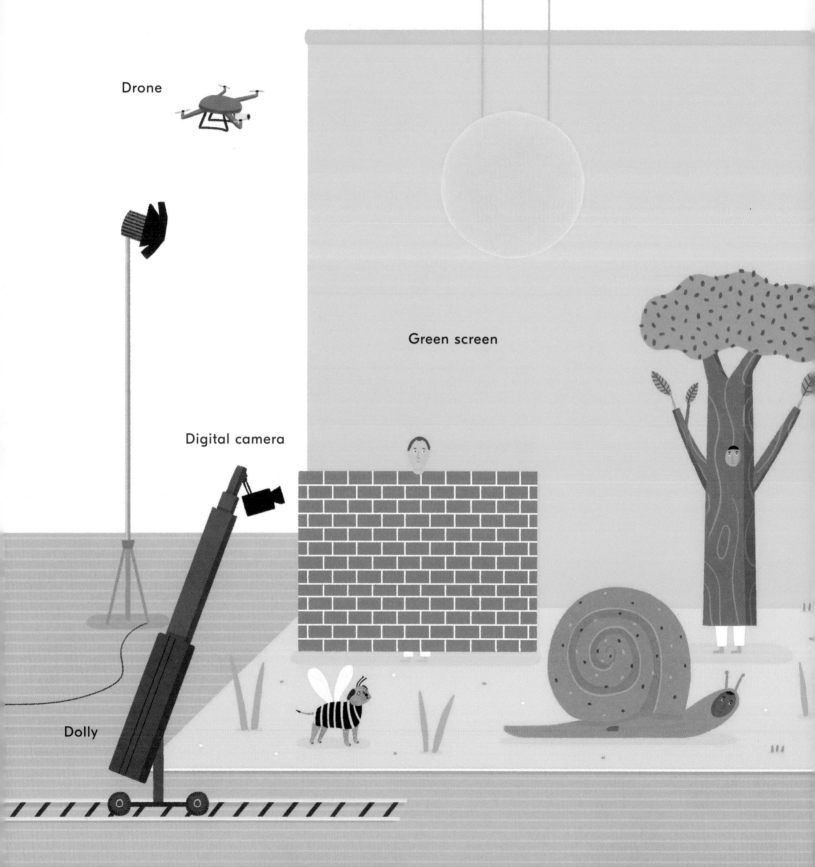

Drone

Green screen

Digital camera

Dolly

There are many parts to my work: I write the script, sew the costumes, select the performers, make the sets, film all the scenes, and then edit everything together.

Spotlight

Action camera

I am a video artist.

I am an artist who speaks my mind. When I was a kid, I used to put signs on my door to express myself — it all started there! I use the power of art to draw people's attention to things I want to change, like the way we care for the environment and how we treat each other.

Peace sign

Globe

Notebooks

Laptop

Placards

Research library

People can hang my artwork on their walls or carry it around to stand up for what they think is right. I hope they'll make their own messages as well!

I am an activist artist.

I am an artist who hated math in school, but now I use it for every piece I make. I need to take very precise measurements, but I also have to respond to all the patterns, swirls, and holes in the wood.

I love combining the familiar with the magical; I take once-living material and give it new life. I just have to be careful around the sharp tools!

I am a woodworker.

Sawdust

Table saw

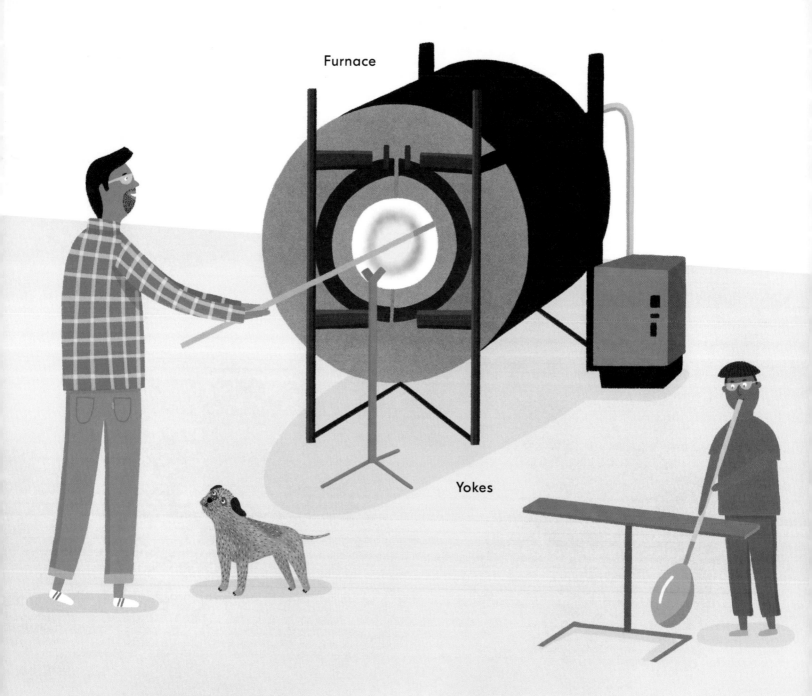

Furnace

Yokes

I am an artist who likes chemical reactions. I can take a very hot liquid, blow air into it, and then wait for it to cool down and become a solid piece of glass. It *blows* my mind every time! A lot of what I make is unpredictable, like where the shapes end up or how they react to light. It isn't easy though: the room is hot, the work is dangerous, and the smells are bad.

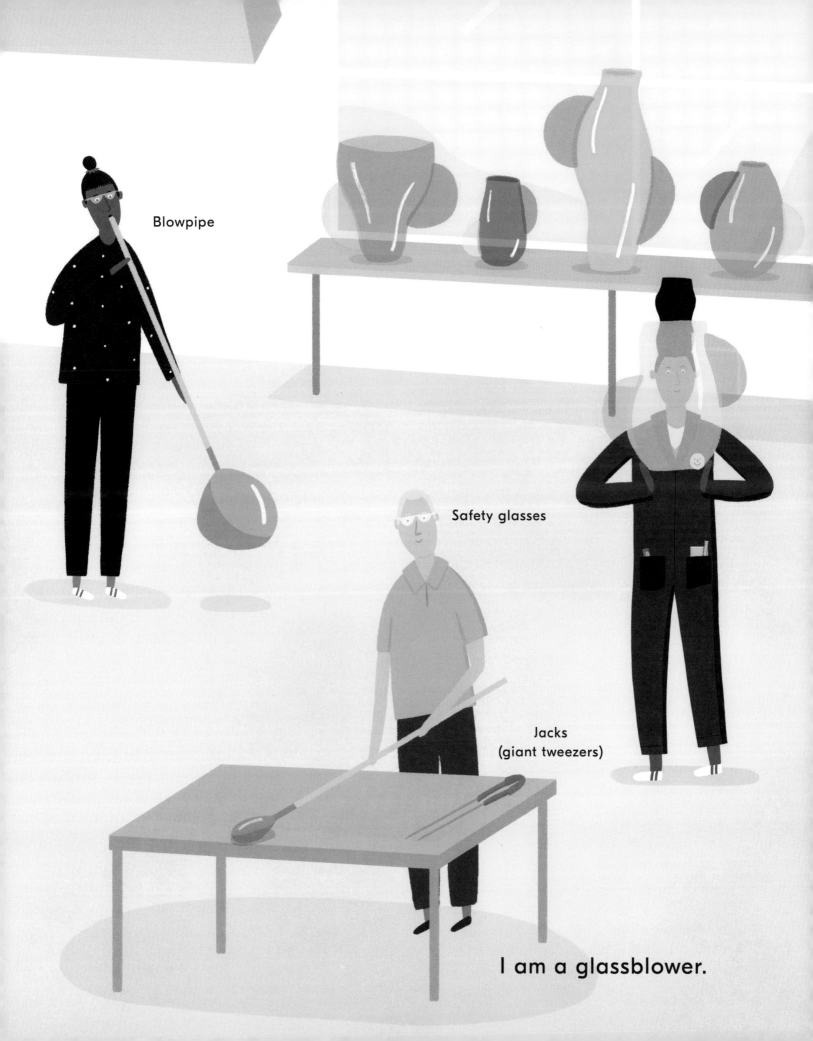

Blowpipe

Safety glasses

Jacks
(giant tweezers)

I am a glassblower.

I am an artist who values tradition and community.

Thread

Needle

I take old clothes, scraps, and rags from loved ones, friends, and neighbors and sew them together to tell a story or make a statement. My mother taught me how to sew and quilt. As my thoughts travel with the needle and thread, I feel a sense of calm.

Fabric

I am a textile artist.

We are artists who take clay that is soft, wet, and squishy and sculpt it into something hard and solid. We can mold it while it spins on a wheel or build up shapes by hand. The pieces go into the kiln—a very hot oven that hardens the clay—and then we decorate the hardened pieces with glaze and other things and fire them again. It's always a surprise to see them when they come out!

Glazes

Clay

Pottery wheel

Drying shelves

Water buckets

Glaze table

Kiln

We are ceramicists.

I am an artist who is obsessed with nature. Have you ever thought about how many things are around us that we don't truly notice? Nature gives me all the art materials I need.

Trees

Grass

Rocks

Branches

Leaves

There is so much beauty in a rock that has been smoothed by the ocean or an icicle that has formed on a tree. I draw inspiration from nature and use it as a starting point for my creations.

I am an environmental artist.

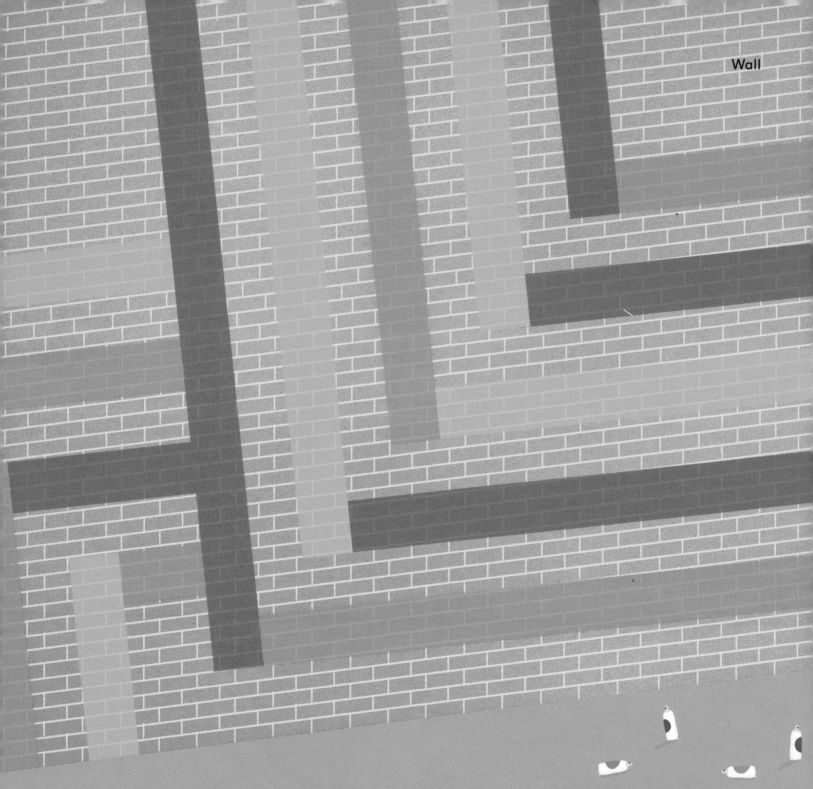

We are artists who want to make the city beautiful with art everyone can see. Using simple materials that we can carry with us, like spray paint and stencils, we make art in places that people don't normally pay attention to, like tunnels, stairwells, and empty walls. Working in the street means that the city becomes our museum.

Mask

Backpack

Portable ladder

Spray paint

Stereo

We are street artists, also known as graffiti artists.

I am an artist who works with words
and ideas. I am a text artist.

I am an artist who likes to look at
the world. I am a landscape painter.

I am an artist who likes to work with
small bits to make a big picture. I am
a mosaicist.

I am an artist who is obsessed with everyday objects. I am a pop artist.

I am an artist who doesn't follow the rules. I am an abstract painter.

I am an artist who uses words, props, and my own body. I am a performance artist.

I am an artist who uses something you can't touch to make a sculpture. I am a light artist.

I am an artist who wears what I make. I am a jeweler.

So, really, anything can be art? Art can be made out of paint or glass, wood or fabric, words or rocks. Art can even be mostly ideas or feelings.

Exactly, it's all about making something you want to share or making something because you enjoy it.

I think part of being an artist is having fun and seeing where an idea or a material can take you. I like that you can mix any of these techniques together. I love making art!

Me too! It has been really nice to try out different styles and materials. I'm excited to use some of the techniques we learned from artists today. Inspiration can come from so many places.

It has been so much fun meeting these artists today. Thank you all!

I Am an Artist
by Doro Globus and Rose Blake

Published by
David Zwirner Books
520 West 20th Street, 2nd Floor
New York, New York 10011
+ 1 212 727 2070
davidzwirnerbooks.com

Design: A Practice for Everyday Life, London
Project editor: Jessica Palinski Hoos
Proofreader: Elizabeth Gordon
Production manager: Felicity Awdry
Color separations: Altaimage
Printing: LEGO, SrL

Typefaces: Alwa Display and GT Eesti Display
Paper: Magno Natural, 170gsm

Publication © 2024 David Zwirner Books
Text © 2024 Doro Globus
Illustrations © 2024 Rose Blake

All rights reserved. No part of this book may
be reproduced or transmitted in any form or by
any means, electronic or mechanical, including
photographing, recording, or information storage
and retrieval, without prior permission in writing
from the publisher.

ISBN 978-1-64423-121-0
Library of Congress Control Number: 2023942039

Printed in Italy

Scan to access the *I Am an Artist* curriculum guide
and activity packet!

When Rose and I talked about our next book,
we knew we wanted to explore what an artist is and
why people become artists. Thank you, first, to all
the artists who put their work out into the world and
share their voice.

Thank you to Dorothea, who loves making art,
and to Tristan, who cheers us on. Thanks to all
the children who read drafts of this book, especially
Lucia and Madeline. Thank you to our families for
encouraging us and to everyone who read, bought,
or sold *Making a Great Exhibition*.

Thank you to the team behind the book: Anne Wehr
for her wise guidance, Jess Palinski Hoos for her
enthusiasm, and Elizabeth Gordon for her sharp eye.
For believing in the project, thank you to Susan
Cernek and David and Lucas Zwirner. Thank you
to A Practice for Everyday Life, and to Felicity Awdry,
Sara Chan, Luke Chase, Amy Hordes, James Spackman,
Molly Stein, Jules Thomson, and Joey Young.

Most of all, thank you to Rose Blake for her
friendship, her talent, her voice.